THE WORLD'S TOP TEN

OCEANS
AND SEAS

Neil Morris

Illustrated by Vanessa Card

Chrysalis Children's Books

Words in **bold** are explained in the glossary
on pages 30–31.

This edition published in 2003 by
Chrysalis Children's Books
The Chrysalis Building, Bramley Road,
London W10 6SP

Editor: Maria O'Neill
Designer: Dawn Apperley
Picture Researcher: Diana Morris
Consultant: Elizabeth M Lewis

Printed in China By Imago

Picture acknowledgements:
Bryan & Cherry Alexander: 14, 15, 17, 29t. J Allan Cash: 5b,
11t, 13, 16, 18, 19, 20. Bruce Coleman: 23 Dr. Eckart Pott,
29b Hans Reinhard. Eye Ubiquitous: 12 David Cumming.
James Davis Photography: 8. Robert Harding Picture Library:
9t. Hutchison Library: 26. FLPA: 21 Panda/M Melodia,
22 S McCutcheon. Christine Osborne: 28t. Planet Earth: 25.
SPL: 4 Tom van Sant/Geosphere Project. Tony Stone Images:
10 Trip: 28b R Cracknell. Zefa: 24, 27.

ISBN 1 84138 486 0

British Library Cataloguing in Publication Data for this book
is available from the British Library.

Contents

What are oceans and seas?

An ocean is a huge stretch of salt water. Four oceans lie around the world's **continents**, and their waters cover more than two-thirds of the Earth's surface. Seas are smaller stretches of salt water that form parts of oceans. A sea is often partly surrounded by land and is usually connected to an ocean by **channels**. If it has a wide, curving shoreline, a sea is sometimes called a gulf or a bay.

This picture shows the vast size of the biggest ocean in the world, the Pacific. The white, frozen ocean at the top is the Arctic. The picture was put together by computer from thousands of photographs taken from space satellites.

Watery planet

The Earth formed about 4600 million years ago. Early in the planet's life, steam from **volcanoes** fell back to its surface as rain. The rain collected into huge pools and then formed one big ocean, surrounding a vast mass of land.

Over millions of years, the land split and moved apart to form the separate continents. This movement divided the great stretch of water into all the different oceans and seas that we know today.

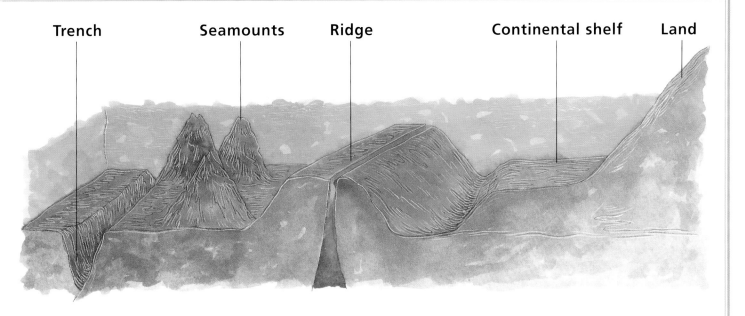

Trench   Seamounts   Ridge   Continental shelf   Land

Beneath the sea

Ocean floors make up parts of the Earth's outer layer of rocks, called the **crust**. The crust is cracked into huge pieces, called **plates**, that fit together like a giant jigsaw puzzle. The plates move just a few centimetres each year, making mountains and valleys on the sea bed, just as they do on dry land.

Mountain ranges under the sea are usually called ridges, and valleys are called trenches. There are single mountain peaks, too, called seamounts. Many of the world's islands are the tops of underwater mountains.

The biggest oceans and seas

In this book we take a look at the world's biggest stretches of water. These are the four oceans and the six largest seas. We see how different they are from each other and learn about the people and animals who live in and around them.

Norfolk and Philip Islands lie in the Pacific Ocean, about 1400 kilometres east of Australia. They are both part of a ridge that runs along the ocean floor from the north of New Zealand.

The biggest oceans and seas

The map shows the ten biggest oceans and seas in the world, surrounding the seven continents. The deep blue areas on the map show where the oceans are very deep. The Pacific Ocean is split in two on the map, so that we can see the round Earth as a flat shape. The South China Sea, Bering Sea and Sea of Okhotsk are all parts of the Pacific Ocean. The Caribbean Sea, Mediterranean Sea and Gulf of Mexico belong to the Atlantic Ocean. At the southern end of the world the Pacific, Atlantic and Indian Oceans meet around the frozen continent of Antarctica.

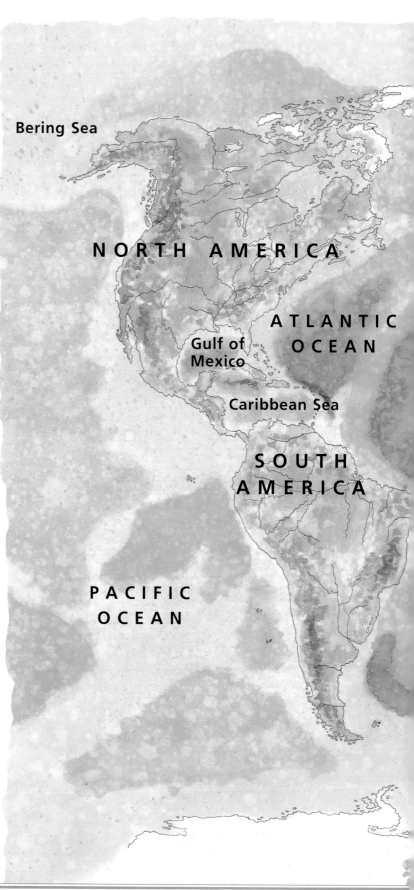

The world's top ten oceans and seas

1 Pacific Ocean	181 200 000	sq km
2 Atlantic Ocean	106 480 000	sq km
3 Indian Ocean	74 060 000	sq km
4 Arctic Ocean	13 230 000	sq km
5 South China Sea	2 974 600	sq km
6 Caribbean Sea	2 753 000	sq km
7 Mediterranean Sea	2 503 000	sq km
8 Bering Sea	2 268 180	sq km
9 Gulf of Mexico	1 542 985	sq km
10 Sea of Okhotsk	1 527 570	sq km

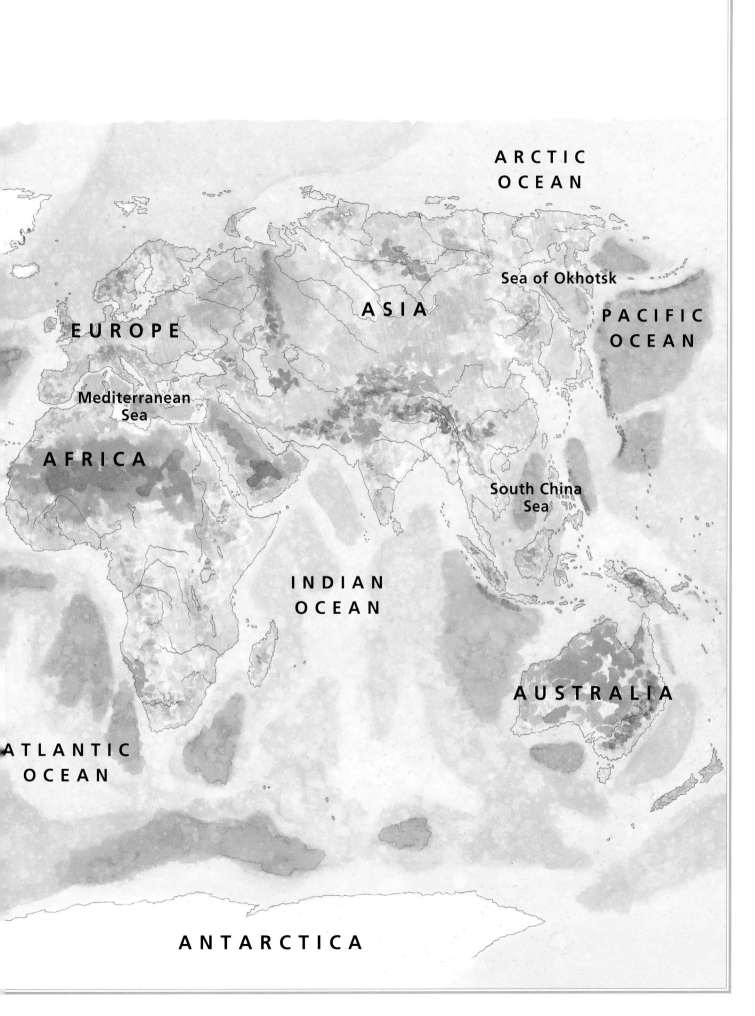

ARCTIC
OCEAN

Sea of Okhotsk

ASIA

PACIFIC
OCEAN

EUROPE

Mediterranean
Sea

AFRICA

South China
Sea

INDIAN
OCEAN

AUSTRALIA

ATLANTIC
OCEAN

ANTARCTICA

Pacific Ocean

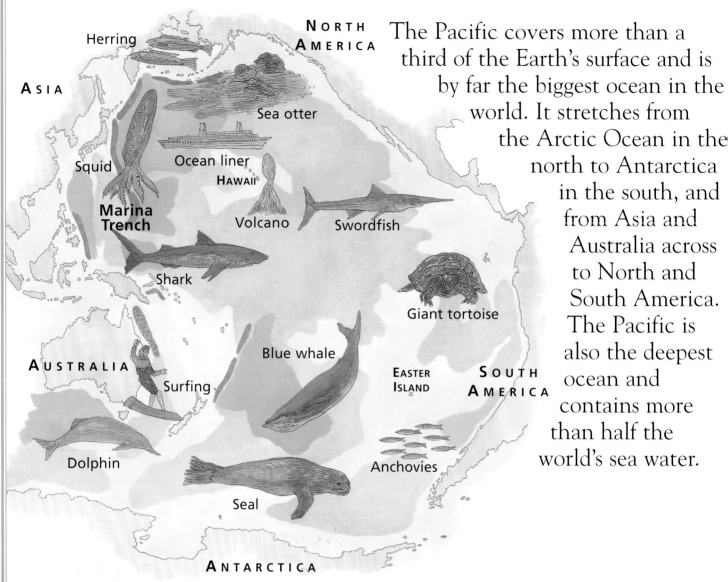

Herring

NORTH AMERICA

ASIA

Sea otter

Squid

Ocean liner

HAWAII

Marina Trench

Volcano

Swordfish

Shark

Giant tortoise

AUSTRALIA

Surfing

Blue whale

EASTER ISLAND

SOUTH AMERICA

Dolphin

Seal

Anchovies

ANTARCTICA

The Pacific covers more than a third of the Earth's surface and is by far the biggest ocean in the world. It stretches from the Arctic Ocean in the north to Antarctica in the south, and from Asia and Australia across to North and South America. The Pacific is also the deepest ocean and contains more than half the world's sea water.

People of the Pacific

The Pacific is dotted with more than 25 000 islands. The original people of the islands of Hawaii are Polynesians. Historians believe that the Polynesians were the first people to explore the Pacific. They sailed from South East Asia more than 2000 years ago and travelled over a huge area of the ocean, from Hawaii to New Zealand, and right across to Easter Island.

The people of the island kingdom of Tonga are Polynesians. Traditionally they row across the blue Pacific waters in ocean-going canoes.

Crossing the ocean

In 1521 a Portuguese explorer, Ferdinand Magellan, became the first European to sail across this great ocean. It was a calm voyage, from the tip of South America to the Philippines. Magellan's three ships were driven across the warm waters by gentle winds, and so he named the ocean Pacific, which means 'peaceful'. But its waters are not always like this. Violent storms often blow across the surface. During one Pacific storm, waves on the open sea were measured at up to 34 metres high.

The rocky coast of Oregon, one of the Pacific states of the United States of America. If you sailed west from here, you would cross 8000 kilometres of ocean and arrive in Japan.

FACTS

AREA	181 200 000 sq km
AVERAGE DEPTH	4188 m
DEEPEST POINT	11022 m, Mariana Trench

Greatest depth

The deepest point on Earth lies near the Pacific island of Guam. Oceanographers – scientists who study the oceans – have named this spot Challenger Deep. It is the lowest part of the Mariana Trench, a curving valley on the sea bed. In 1960 the **submersible** *Trieste* made a world-record dive to a depth of 10 916 metres inside the trench.

In the past, ships let down cables to measure depth. Now this is usually done by sonar equipment, which sends out pulses of sound. These bounce off the sea bed, and the echoes are measured to make a map of the sea floor.

Atlantic Ocean

The Atlantic is just over half as big as the Pacific Ocean. It lies on the eastern side of North and South America, and its other boundary is formed by Europe and Africa. The part of the ocean north of the **Equator** is sometimes called the North Atlantic. South of the Equator is the part known as the South Atlantic.

Continental shelf

The sea bed around the edges of oceans, where the water is shallow, is called the **continental shelf**. Around the Atlantic, the shelf lies less than 150 metres below the surface. The island of Newfoundland, the Falkland Islands and the British Isles all lie on the Atlantic's continental shelf. Its shallow waters are the ocean's best fishing grounds and a third of the world's total catch is made in the Atlantic.

NORTH AMERICA

ICELAND

Walrus **NEWFOUNDLAND**

Oi

Puffin

AZORES

Cod

EUROP

SARGASSO SEA

Lobster

PUERTO RICO TRENCH

Eel

AFRICA

Barracuda

EQUATOR

Green turtle

Pilchards

SOUTH AMERICA

Killer whale

MID-ATLANTIC RIDGE

FALKLAND ISLANDS

Penguin

Fishing on the stormy Atlantic seas. A part of the continental shelf off Newfoundland, called the Grand Banks, makes specially good fishing grounds.

Mid-Atlantic Ridge

The Atlantic Ocean started to form about 150 million years ago, as the continents drifted apart. It is still getting wider, by about 2.5 centimetres every year. As the American and African plates move apart, **molten** rock from inside the Earth is forming a great mountain range under the Atlantic. The Mid-Atlantic Ridge runs from north to south and has mountains up to 4000 metres high. Most peaks are more than 2000 metres below the surface, but in some places they jut out of the water, forming islands.

FACTS

AREA	106 480 000 sq km
AVERAGE DEPTH	3736 m
DEEPEST POINT	9460 m, Puerto Rico Trench

These rocks jut out of the ocean off São Miguel, one of the nine islands that make up the Azores. The islands lie on the slopes of the Mid-Atlantic Ridge and are often shaken by earthquakes.

Sea within the ocean

The Sargasso Sea is a large area of calm water in the western part of the North Atlantic. This sea within the ocean gets its name from the huge patches of green sargassum weed that float on its surface.

In autumn the Sargasso Sea becomes the breeding ground for millions of European and North American eels. When the eggs hatch, the tiny eels drift with the **currents**. It takes them up to three years to reach the coast. Then the young eels, called elvers, swim into rivers in Europe and North America. Years later, the adult eels swim back to the Sargasso Sea to breed and then die.

11

Indian Ocean

The third largest ocean, the Indian, stretches from Africa to Australia, covering almost 10 000 kilometres at its widest point. It meets the two larger oceans near Antarctica, and narrows to the north around India. Arab, Chinese and Indian trading ships have all sailed across the Indian Ocean since ancient times.

A row of boats on the muddy waters of the Ganges **delta**, in Bangladesh. Together with the River Brahmaputra, the Ganges forms the largest delta in the world, 360 kilometres across.

Filling the ocean

Water **evaporates** from all the world's oceans and seas, and forms clouds which fall back to Earth as rain. Much of the rain that falls on land flows back to the sea as rivers. This cycle waters the world's continents and keeps the oceans full.

The Indian Ocean has an unusual water cycle. In summer, warm **monsoon** winds blow right across the ocean towards India, carrying a huge amount of **water vapour**. As these winds rise to cross the Himalayan mountains, they cool and clouds form. Torrential rain falls on India, filling the river systems quickly. Low-lying areas become flooded as the water races back to the ocean.

The Ganges fan

The Indian flood water carries vast amounts of mud and rocks with it. Much of it flows into the River Ganges which carries this **sediment** towards the ocean. The river drops its load of mud on the sea floor near the river's **mouth**. This sediment forms layers hundreds of metres thick. Underwater **avalanches** then spread the sediment into a fan shape, called the Ganges fan, which stretches for thousands of kilometres under the Indian Ocean.

The island of Madagascar has warm, palm-fringed beaches. In the southern Indian Ocean, currents move in an **anti-clockwise** direction, flowing down the channel between Madagascar and Africa.

FACTS

AREA	74 060 000 sq km
AVERAGE DEPTH	3872 m
DEEPEST POINT	7542 m, Java Trench

Prehistoric fish

In 1938 a fisherman caught a very unusual fish in the Indian Ocean off southern Africa. He took it to a museum, where scientists realized that it was a coelacanth – a fish they thought had died out about 70 million years ago! It was a further 14 years before another coelacanth was caught, but since then many have been found. They grow up to two metres long, and the female gives birth to live young rather than laying eggs.

Arctic Ocean

The Arctic is the smallest and shallowest of the world's four oceans. It lies around the North Pole, to the north of Europe, North America and Asia. This ocean is almost surrounded by land, and it is about 4500 kilometres across at its widest point, between Alaska and Norway.

Most Arctic icebergs drift south with the currents and melt in warmer seas. Icebergs are much bigger than they look: only about a seventh of their ice appears above the water.

ALASKA

ASIA

Walrus

Beluga whale

NORTH AMERICA

Seal

Arctic tern

Eider duck

ANGARA BASIN
NORTH POLE

ELLESMERE ISLAND

Polar bear

Narwhal

GREENLAND

Inuit

Icebergs

Guillemot

NORWAY

Sperm whale

ICELAND

EUROPE

Frozen ocean

The Arctic Ocean freezes up to 50 metres thick during the winter months. Even in summer the centre is covered in this polar ice, up to two metres thick. **Pack ice** forms around the edges of the polar ice, where it is constantly broken up and pushed together again by the movement of water beneath it.

Huge **icebergs** float around the edges of the Arctic. Most of them break off from the **glaciers** and **ice shelves** of Greenland, the world's biggest island.

To the North Pole

As long ago as the fourth century BC, the Greek explorer Pytheas sailed to the edge of the Arctic region. Yet until recently, many people believed that there was land, rather than frozen sea, at the North Pole. In 1893 a Norwegian scientist, Fridtjof Nansen, led an expedition to study the Arctic. His ship drifted with the ice for three years, but did not get to the Pole. In 1909, US naval officer Robert Peary, with an American assistant and four **Inuit** men, reached the Pole on foot, from their base on Ellesmere Island.

Today, submarines can travel under the ice to reach the Pole and aeroplanes regularly fly over it.

An Inuit fisherman has dug a hole in the ice to fish for cod. The ice melts and gets thinner in summer.

Life in the Arctic

The Inuit people live around the Arctic coasts of Canada, Alaska and Greenland. Lapps live along the northern coasts of Scandinavia. Both peoples traditionally hunted and fished to survive.

Seals and walrus live here, feeding on Arctic fish. Whales swim in the region, including the tusked narwhal and the white beluga whale. Blue whales, the largest creatures that have ever lived, visit the Arctic in summer to feed and breed. Polar bears follow the shifting ice in search of their favourite food – seals.

FACTS

AREA	13 230 000 sq km
AVERAGE DEPTH	1330 m
DEEPEST POINT	5570 m, Angara Basin

South China Sea

The South China Sea is part of the Pacific Ocean. As a separate stretch of water, it is the largest sea in the world, smaller only than the four oceans. It has the southern coast of China, Vietnam and the Malay **Peninsula** to the west, the Philippines to the east, and the island of Borneo to the south.

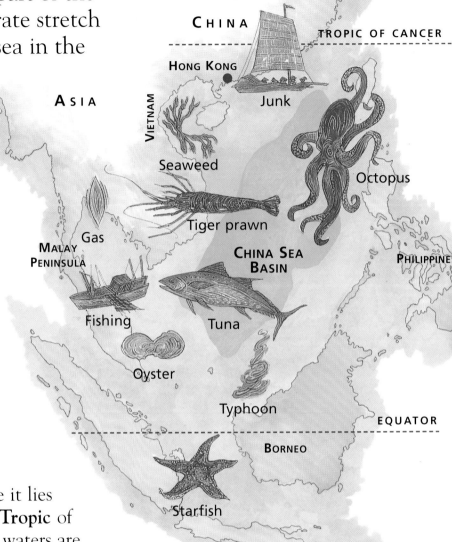

Typhoons

This sea is truly **tropical**, since it lies between the Equator and the **Tropic** of Cancer. In summer its surface waters are warmed up to 29°C. This high sea temperature can cause warm, moist air to rise, creating spiralling, stormy winds and torrential rainstorms. In the Far East these hurricane conditions are known as typhoons, from the Chinese for 'great winds'.

The South China Sea and nearby Pacific regions have about 25 typhoons every year between May and December.

These ships were wrecked on the island of Luzon by a typhoon. Luzon, the largest island of the Philippines, is often exposed to violent storms.

Hong Kong

One of the world's greatest ports lies on the South China coast. Hong Kong's sheltered harbours were built to protect ships from typhoons.

The sheltered harbours are very important because large numbers of Hong Kong's people live in crowded conditions on the thousands of boats, called sampans and **junks**, that float on the harbour waters.

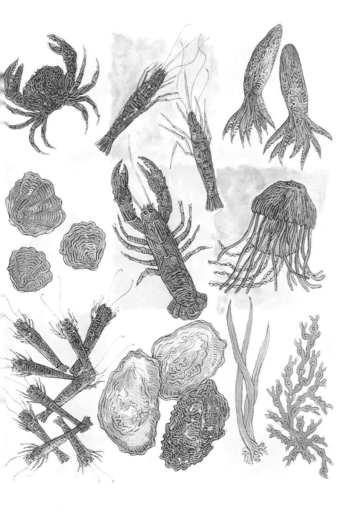

Causeway Bay typhoon shelter, on Hong Kong island, is like a floating town. Junks, sampans and motor launches are moored here, overlooked by offices and apartment blocks.

FACTS

AREA	2 974 600 sq km
AVERAGE DEPTH	1200 m
DEEPEST POINT	5015 m, China Sea Basin

Farming the sea

People now farm the sea as well as the land. In Hong Kong and other parts of the South China Sea, giant tiger prawns are kept in ponds near the shore. They are fed on special **algae** so that they grow quickly, and can easily be hauled in with nets. Oysters are farmed on poles and ropes in sea ponds, where they can be protected from fish that would otherwise eat them. The Chinese also cultivate seaweed for food.

17

Caribbean Sea

The Caribbean Sea is surrounded by the islands of the West Indies to the north and east. The South American countries of Colombia and Venezuela lie to the south, with Central America to the west. The sea was named after the Carib Indians, who were the islands' first inhabitants.

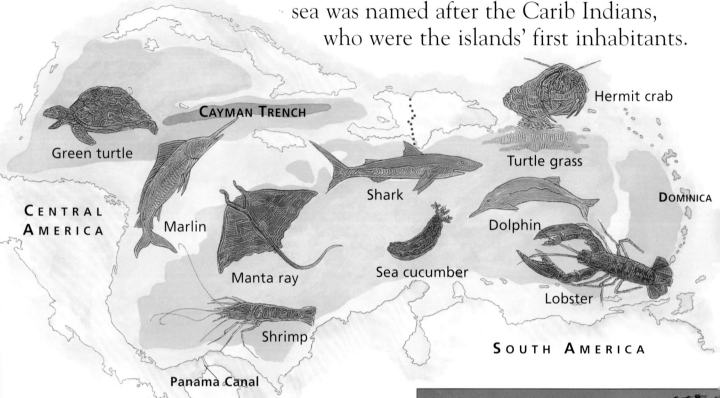

Hermit crab

CAYMAN TRENCH

Green turtle

Turtle grass

Shark

CENTRAL AMERICA

Marlin

Dolphin

DOMINICA

Manta ray

Sea cucumber

Lobster

Shrimp

SOUTH AMERICA

Panama Canal

Pirates and buccaneers

For hundreds of years the Caribbean Sea was a dangerous place to sail. Christopher Columbus reached the Caribbean islands in 1492. He sailed in search of gold, and many of the Europeans who went after him did the same. Pirates hid around the islands, ready to attack the Spanish **galleons** and rob them of their treasure. The pirates came to be known as buccaneers, from the boucan, or wooden grill, on which they smoked their meat.

Columbus named the rugged, forested and mountainous island of Dominica in 1493, on his second voyage to the **New World**.

Treasures of the sea

About one seventh of the world's **coral reefs** lie in Caribbean waters. The tropical sea is an ideal home for many other creatures, including the West Indian manatee. This large, slow-moving mammal belongs to a group of animals called sea cows. It can stay underwater for up to 15 minutes, feeding on seaweed. It then comes to the surface to breathe air. Unfortunately the manatee is being threatened by changes to the Caribbean coastline as trade and tourism increase.

Panama Canal

Some of the busiest shipping routes in the world pass through the Caribbean Sea. This is mainly due to the position of the Panama **Canal**, which links the Atlantic and Pacific Oceans. The opening of this canal in 1914 meant that ships no longer had to sail around the southern tip of South America to get from one ocean to the other. Instead they can travel just 81 kilometres along the canal which crosses the narrow country of Panama.

FACTS

AREA	2 753 000 sq km
AVERAGE DEPTH	2400 m
DEEPEST POINT	7680 m, Cayman Trench

A ship approaches one of the Panama Canal's six pairs of locks. The lock fills up with water so that the ship can sail in. Then the lock empties, taking the ship down to a lower level.

Mediterranean Sea

The world's third biggest sea is the Mediterranean. Its name means 'in the middle of land', and it is almost **landlocked** between the continents of Europe, Africa and Asia. In the west the narrow **Strait** of Gibraltar links the Mediterranean to the Atlantic Ocean.

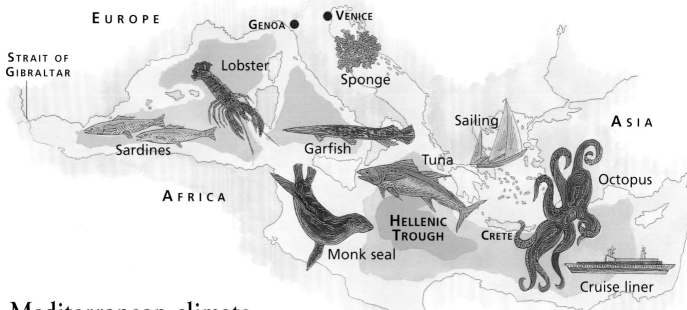

Mediterranean climate

The deeper Mediterranean waters vary little in temperature throughout the year. Near the surface, the water is very warm in summer, sometimes reaching 27°C. In winter it never gets too cold, and the same is true of the land bordering the sea.

Strong winds can sweep across the Mediterranean Sea. Sometimes, a hot, dry wind called the sirocco blows from the Sahara Desert and can raise air temperatures to over 40°C. At other times, cooler weather is brought by the mistral, a cold wind blowing down from the Alps, Europe's highest mountains.

Holidaymakers flock to the sandy coasts of the Mediterranean to enjoy the sunshine and the sea. This beach is at Oludeniz, in Turkey.

Great civilizations

Many early civilizations, including those of Egypt, Greece and Rome, developed along the shores of the Mediterranean. About 5000 years ago, the **Minoan Civilization** developed on the island of Crete, which today belongs to Greece.

Even after the fall of the Roman Empire in the 5th century AD, the Mediterranean remained the greatest sea route in the world. **City-states** based on the ports of Venice and Genoa grew into important centres of trade. Christopher Columbus was born in Genoa in 1451. He made his first voyages along the Mediterranean coast when he was 14 years old.

Oil barrels washed up on the shore near Genoa which, today, is Italy's leading port.

Modern problems

The world's seas have been used as dumping grounds for many years. By the 1970s water **pollution** had become a serious problem in the Mediterranean. Most pollution was caused by oil, from ships and industry, and sewage. Tourists cause problems too. They have taken over the breeding beaches of the Mediterranean monk seal, reducing the seal population to just a few hundred.

FACTS

AREA	2 503 000 sq km
AVERAGE DEPTH	1485 m
DEEPEST POINT	5093 m, Hellenic Trough

Bering Sea

The Bering Sea is the most northerly part of the Pacific Ocean. It lies between Siberia, which belongs to Russia, and Alaska, which belongs to the United States of America. It is connected to the Arctic Ocean by the Bering Strait.

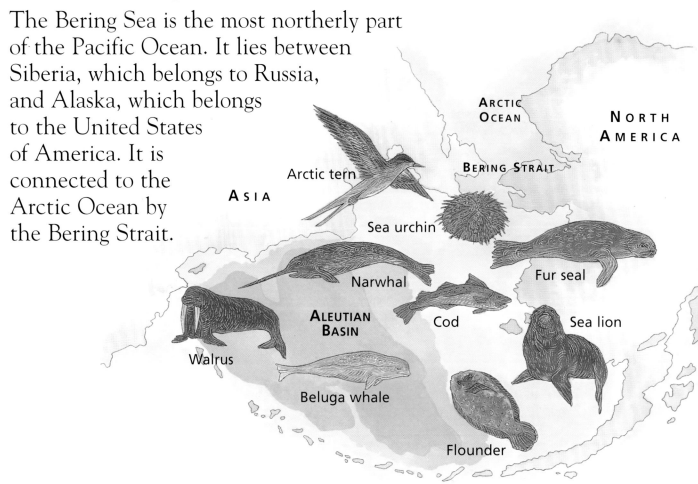

ARCTIC OCEAN

NORTH AMERICA

BERING STRAIT

Arctic tern

ASIA

Sea urchin

Fur seal

Narwhal

Cod

Sea lion

Walrus

ALEUTIAN BASIN

Beluga whale

Flounder

Asia meets North America

The Bering Strait, between north-east Asia and north-west America, is only 88 kilometres wide. It is a shallow channel, with a greatest depth of 52 metres. But it was not always like this. During the **Ice Age**, the sea level fell by hundreds of metres. This made a land bridge between the two continents and, in prehistoric times, tens of thousands of years ago, hunters in search of food crossed from Asia. They were the ancestors of all the native American peoples.

The town of Nome, on the Alaska coast, began as an Inuit settlement but grew quickly after gold was discovered there in 1899.

Vitus Bering

In 1725 Peter the Great, the Tsar of Russia, sent a Danish sailor, named Vitus Bering, to find out if there was a land bridge between Asia and America. Three years after leaving St Petersburg, Bering reached the strait that was later named after him. Heavy fog prevented him from seeing the coast of Alaska, but he assumed, rightly, that Asia and America were not joined.

In 1733 Bering returned to the region, and this time he did find the Alaskan coast. But on the return voyage to Siberia he fell ill and died. The island where his ship finally anchored was also named after him.

Hunting to extinction

In 1741 sailors discovered a huge sea mammal in the Bering Sea. Steller's sea cow, related to the manatee of the Caribbean, was up to 9 metres long and weighed as much as 6 tonnes. It was hunted for its meat, but so many were killed that within 30 years they had died out. The same could have happened to northern fur seals, which breed each year on the beaches of the Pribilof Islands, south-west of Alaska. International agreements have now stopped the slaughtering of these animals.

FACTS

AREA	2 268 180 sq km
AVERAGE DEPTH	1400 m
DEEPEST POINT	5121, Aleutian Basin

Northern fur seals feed on fish and squid. They rarely come to land outside the breeding season. Males can weigh five times as much as females, who usually give birth to a single pup each year.

Gulf of Mexico

The Gulf of Mexico is the largest gulf in the world. It is linked to the Atlantic Ocean by the Straits of Florida. The Gulf stretches across the Tropic of Cancer. Its coastline is formed by the United States of America and Mexico, and it is separated from the Caribbean Sea by the island of Cuba.

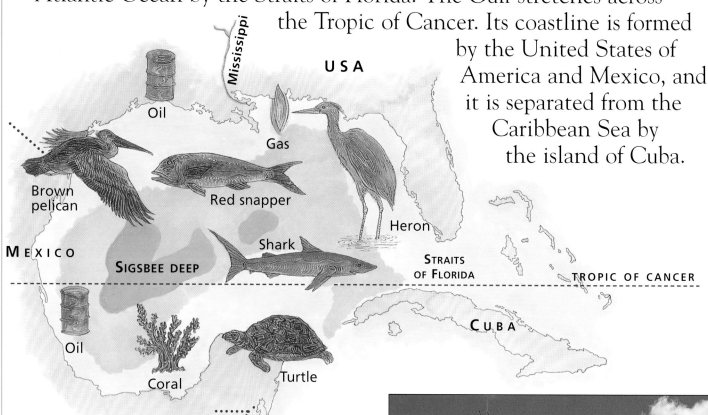

Mississippi

Oil

USA

Gas

Brown pelican

Red snapper

Heron

MEXICO

SIGSBEE DEEP

Shark

STRAITS OF FLORIDA

TROPIC OF CANCER

Oil

Coral

Turtle

CUBA

Florida Current

In the Atlantic Ocean there is a strong flow of warm water, called the North Equatorial Current. It flows across the Caribbean Sea, through the Yucatan Channel into the Gulf of Mexico, where it is known as the Florida Current. It flows **clockwise** around the Gulf and out through the Straits of Florida. Once past the islands of the Bahamas, it joins another current to become the famous Gulf Stream and moves back across the Atlantic.

The harbour at Key West is at the end of a chain of coral islands called the Florida Keys. Boating and deep-sea fishing are popular throughout the Keys.

This waterspout was photographed near the Florida Keys. These watery storms rarely last for longer than 15 minutes.

FACTS

AREA	1 542 985 sq km
AVERAGE DEPTH	1500 m
DEEPEST POINT	5203 m, Sigsbee Deep

Waterspouts

Violent storms often hit the Gulf between June and October. Sometimes, as a storm blows over the sea, it forms a waterspout. This is a spinning funnel of air that hangs from the base of a thundercloud. When the whirling wind gets near the surface of the sea, it makes the water bulge up under it. Then it sucks up a column of water droplets. The waterspout may be up to 300 metres wide. It travels across the sea with its thundercloud, and can cause great damage to anything in its path.

Oil and gas

The rocks beneath the Gulf are a big source of oil and natural gas. Oil rigs are set up on the continental shelf off Louisiana and Yucatan, where the water is up to 150 metres deep. The USA is the third biggest producer of oil in the world, and Mexico is the sixth biggest.

Oil production and other industries bring the risk of pollution, and this is a problem for the Gulf's wildlife. Red snappers, flounder and mullet swim in its warm waters. Whooping cranes fly down from Canada to winter here, and the coastal regions are home to green-backed herons.

Sea of Okhotsk

The tenth largest stretch of water in the world, the Sea of Okhotsk, is a northern arm of the Pacific Ocean. It lies mainly off Russian coasts – the mainland of Siberia, the Kamchatka Peninsula, the island of Sakhalin and the Kuril Islands. To the south is Japan's second largest island, Hokkaido. Kamchatka separates the Okhotsk from the Bering Sea.

Gold

GULF OF SHELIKHOV

KAMCHATKA

RUSSIA

MAGADAN ●

Salmon

Klyuchevskaya

Crab

Seals

Herring

Volcanoes

Shrimp

Sperm whale

SAKHALIN

KURIL ISLANDS BASIN

Steller's sea eagle

JAPAN
HOKKAIDO

Siberian coast

Winters are severe in the very north-east of Russia. But when gold and other metals were found here, workers moved to this region. Oil and **natural gas** have also been discovered.

The chief port on the Sea of Okhotsk is Magadan, with a population of 143 000. The town was founded in 1933 around a good harbour and has a naval base. It also has large fish-canning and engineering factories, and there are tin and gold mines nearby.

This area is the homeland of the Yakut, Chukchi and Evenki peoples. Some still live in traditional log huts and herd reindeer.

Near the Okhotsk coast, ice clings to the rocky shore as it melts in the open sea. In winter, the average air temperature is -7°C near the southern coast and -20°C in the north.

Volcanic ranges

The Kamchatka Peninsula is about 1200 kilometres long and has 22 **active** volcanoes. The highest, Klyuchevskaya, rises to 4750 metres. The peninsula leads to a chain of 56 volcanic islands, the Kurils. At least 35 of the volcanoes are active.

Both the peninsula and the islands are part of the 'Ring of Fire', a great circle of volcanoes that stretches right around the Pacific Ocean.

The snow-capped dome of a Kamchatkan volcano.

Fog and ice

The Okhotsk waters are difficult for shipping. In summer there are often heavy fogs, and in winter storms and icebergs are common. The northern part of the sea is covered with ice from October to April. Despite this, there are several fishing ports. The sea has salmon, herring and cod, as well as crabs and shrimps. It is also visited by whales and seals. The sea's currents generally flow anti-clockwise around it, and the biggest tides are in the Gulf of Shelikhov. Here the water rises up to 13 metres from low to high tide.

Scientists think this could be a good site for a tidal power station, where the tides are used to turn **generators** and produce electricity.

The world's oceans and seas

There is an enormous difference in size between the world's top ten oceans and seas. The vast Pacific Ocean is roughly as big as the other three oceans put together. The Pacific Ocean is also a hundred times bigger than number ten on the list, the Sea of Okhotsk. Yet Okhotsk is a major stretch of water, over six times bigger than the Persian Gulf.

Persian Gulf

The Persian Gulf is the second largest gulf in the world, after the Gulf of Mexico. It is surrounded by oil-producing nations, such as Saudi Arabia, Iran and the United Arab Emirates. It is a vital shipping lane for oil tankers.

This oil platform (right) was photographed in the Lower Gulf, off the coast of the United Arab Emirates.

Black Sea

Turkey's largest city, Istanbul, lies on the Bosporus, a narrow strait to the south-west of the Black Sea. Together with two other straits, the Bosporus links the Black Sea with the Mediterranean. The Black Sea lies between Europe and Asia and is fed by two large rivers, the Danube and the Dnieper. The Danube flows from the Black Forest, in Germany, to the Black Sea, which it enters in Romania. The Black Sea covers 462 000 square kilometres.

North Sea

The North Sea is a rich fishing ground, with trawlers, such as the one above, sailing out from ports in Britain, Germany and Scandinavia. In recent years falling fish stocks have led to fishing **restrictions** and many fishing communities have declined. The North Sea has many oil and gas fields beneath its floor. Britain and Norway have mined these fields to become the ninth and tenth biggest producers of **crude oil** in the world.

Hudson Bay

Hudson Bay, in north-east Canada, freezes over from November to July each year. During these months polar bears follow the shifting ice and move down from the Arctic Ocean into the bay, in search of food.

Hudson Bay is the world's largest bay, covering more than 1 232 000 square kilometres. But it is quite shallow, with a greatest depth of 259 metres. The long Hudson Strait connects it to the North Atlantic Ocean.

Glossary

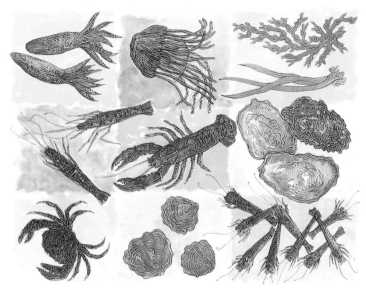

The rich crop of the world's oceans and seas.

active (Of a volcano) that may erupt at any time.

algae A group of tiny plants that includes seaweed.

anti-clockwise In the opposite direction to the movement of a clock's hands.

avalanche A large fall of rocks and mud down a slope.

canal A man-made waterway.

channel A narrow stretch of water connecting oceans and seas.

city-state A self-governing area around a single city, like a small empire.

clockwise In the same direction as the movement of a clock's hands.

continent A huge land mass.

continental shelf The land beneath the sea at the edge of an ocean, where the water is shallow. It is rich in wildlife.

coral reef A large ridge in warm, shallow waters made up of a colony of tiny animals called corals.

crude oil Oil before it has been treated.

crust The Earth's outer shell.

current A strong, steady flow of water in one direction.

delta The fan-shaped area at the mouth of some rivers, where the main flow splits into many smaller channels.

Equator An imaginary circle around the middle of the Earth.

evaporate To change from a liquid to a vapour (or gas).

galleon A large sailing ship with three or more masts, used from the 15th to the 18th centuries.

generator A machine that turns a form of energy, such as the power of water, into electricity.

glacier A slowly moving mass of ice.

Nansen's ship is stuck in the Arctic ice.

Dolphins form part of a Minoan wall picture.

Ice Age A time when a large part of the Earth was covered with ice.

iceberg A mass of ice floating in the sea.

ice shelf A mass of ice floating on the sea and attached to land.

Inuit People of the frozen north region of North America and Greenland.

junk A Chinese sailing boat with square sails.

landlocked Surrounded by land.

Minoan Civilization An ancient society famous for its art and trade.

molten Melted, turned into liquid.

monsoon A seasonal wind that brings heavy rains.

mouth The end of a river, where it flows into the sea.

natural gas Gas that is found under ground and used as fuel.

New World North and South America, which were once new to Europeans.

pack ice Blocks of floating, frozen sea water.

peninsula A strip of land that juts into the sea, almost forming an island.

plate A huge piece of the Earth's shell.

pollution Damage caused by poisonous and harmful substances.

restrictions Rules brought in to make people stick to certain limits.

sediment The load of mud and stones carried by rivers to the sea.

strait A narrow stretch of water between two areas of land.

submersible A submarine (an underwater boat) used to explore the ocean.

tropic One of two imaginary circles around the Earth. The Tropic of Cancer is above the Equator and the Tropic of Capricorn is below it.

tropical Found in the Tropics, the hottest part of the Earth near the Equator.

The submersible, *Trieste*, dives deep in the Pacific Ocean.

volcano An opening where molten rock and gas come from deep inside the Earth.

water vapour Water in the form of a vapour or gas.

Index

Words in **bold** appear in the glossary on pages 30-31.